# Behind the Shadows:

## Volume 1.

# Behind the Shadows: Secrets of the Loa-Hu Wooden-Man. Volume 1.

Dion Hanson. Head Instructor: 5th Degree Black. He has been an inspiration and a life time supporter and friend of the Loa-Hu Kung- Fu fighting system.

Perry Labore: 4th Degree Black. Head of the Colorado area.

Ridge Hanson. 1st Degree Black. Long time friend and assistance Instructor in the Loa-Hu Kung-Fu fighting system.

Mike Nelson. A fellow martial artist who is responsible for bringing me into the Chuan- Lu Kung Fu fighting organization.

Group picture starting from the left. Trevor Jones, Caleb Armstrong, Ben Vandesande, Grand Master Tim Armstrong, Reece Flug, Scott Jones, Hayden Jones, and Travis Jones.

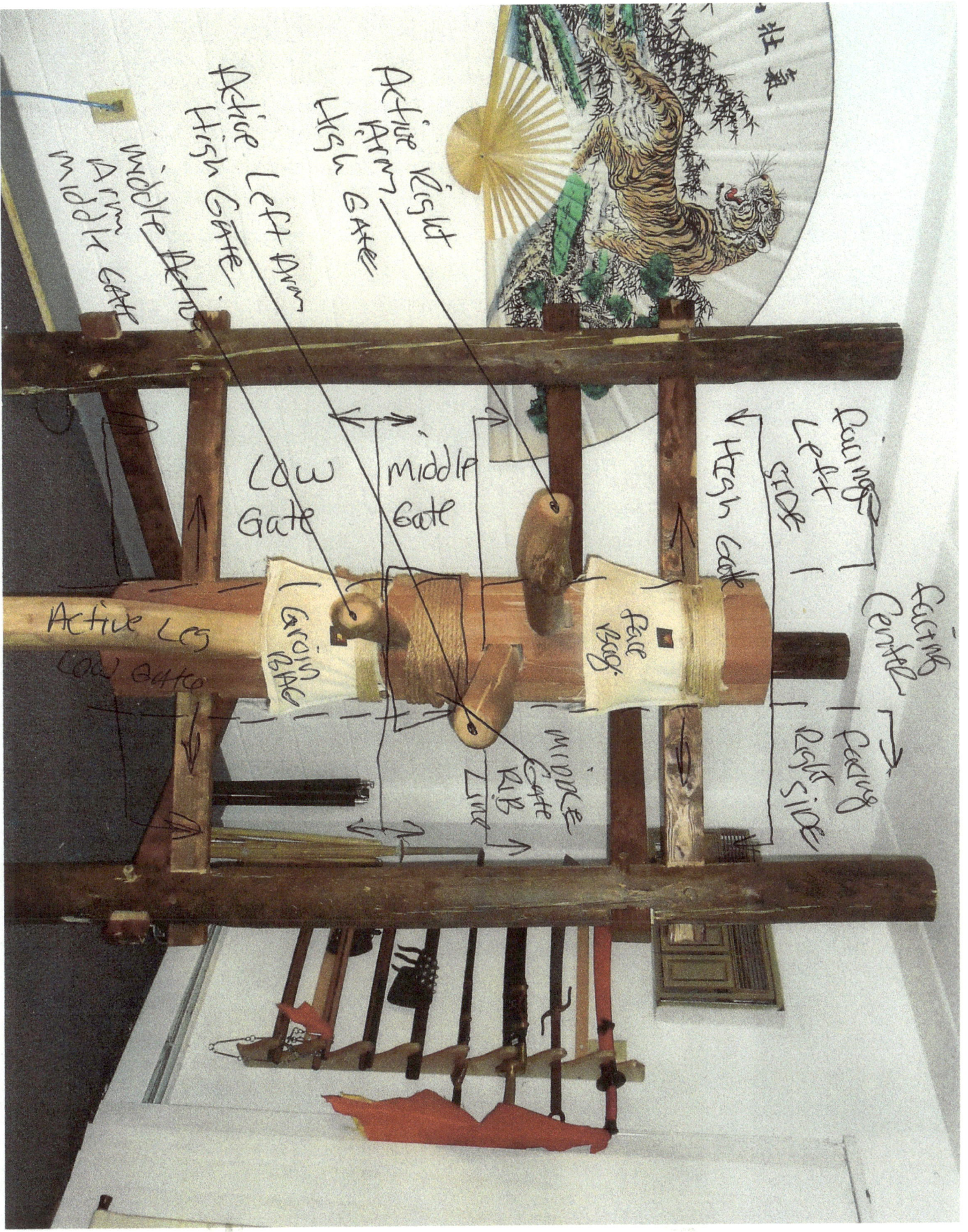

# The Loa-Hu Kung Fu Wooden-Man

The Loa-Hu Kung Fu Wooden-Man is unique and very original. The body is angled for organ strikes—high gate for strikes, middle gate for stomach, and low gate for groin or back leg. The angle is for side of face and the neck line, which is high line. For the ribs, I have rope. So, when you split the rope, you are simulating splitting the ribs. The far back angle represents the kidneys. The body slides right and left to insure you are not attacking too strong—right or left. The body has two bags that are made from canvas and are filled with rock or iron. I recommend starting with rock. If your hands are not seasoned, you will need a product called Dit Da Jow. This will help with your hand conditioning. The bag on top is for a high gate attack. When you hit it, it simulates hitting bone and cartilage. The low gate attack simulates attacking the groin along with nerves in the legs. The frame it sits on is in the form of a triangle with different height adjustments depending on how tall you are or how high you want the body. The adjustments are in six inch increments. The normal heights are five foot, five foot six inches and six foot. The body can fit on any sides. The Wooden-Man is large enough to work out on and yet small enough to fit in any apartment. It has three arms extending nineteen inches from the body. The arms that are attacking are from the high and middle gate, which I call active arms. The Wooden-Man has one leg, which is the leading leg. The body drops down below the leg to simulate the rear or base leg.

# Addressing Wooden-Man in the Loa-Hu Kung-Fu system

Address the Wooden-Man standing five feet from its center in a natural position. Your mind intent should be calm. Look at the Wooden-Man and see all that it has to offer in a martial way. Your left hand should be down—covering the Don-Tein area. Your fingers face to the ground to cover an attack from the low or middle range. Your right hand should cover triple heater (heart), to the bottom of your chin. Your arms should be relaxed and slightly bent. Your legs are in a neutral position with knees slightly bent. Your weight position is 50-50 on both legs.

**1ˢᵗ Move:** After you address the Wooden-Man body, as you would an opponent, swing your left leg in a sweeping motion that will propel your body forward. Your left hand intercepts the Wooden-Man's active left arm, while shifting your whole body left. Your right in, a knife-hand application, strikes the neck bag in the high gate area. Your left foot strikes the Wooden-Man's active leg on the knee joint, or apply a heel hook to the inside of the knee joint area of the active leg. Your right leg acts as a rooted base and stabilizes your body so you can strike in threes. All will do great damage to the Wooden-Man's body.

**2nd Move:** You have to make sure that all moves flow. Try to think of yourself as a flowing creek. Move your blood as it would be a stream throughout your body and feel the power of your natural body's state. Your left leg does a live step back and pulls your right leg to a 50-50 weight stance. Your right foot is in lead position. Your body faces the center of the Wooden-Man's body. Your left hand intercepts the middle active arm as your right hand intercepts the Wooden-Man's left active arm.

**3rd Move:** Un-coil your body. Allow your right hand to drop down the centerline of the Wooden-Man—all the way down the body to a groin strike with your right shoulder placed inside the body's left arm for a guide or block of a high gate attack. When you hit the groin with your right fist, make sure you do a downward tearing motion. Our goal is to tear the groin, not just hit it. Your left hand intercepts the right active arm of the Wooden-Man on the inside of the limb. At the same time, your right knee does a knee strike to the active leg of the Wooden-Man—in the knee joint area. Make sure your foot is turned toward the target and you hit the active leg with the top of your knee. This will insure you do no damage to your own knee.

**4th Move:** Take a live step with left leg to the right side of the Wooden-Man's body and intercept the right active arm with your right forearm. This will free up your left hand for a strike to the face bag in a Tiger Claw position. Hit, grab and pull. At the same time, lift your right foot in a spring like motion and drive said foot downward in a stomping motion on the Wooden-Man's active leg at the knee joint. Your left leg is a rooted base.

**5th Move:** Right foot shoots back to center and maintains a left leg lead. Remember to stay in a 50-50 weighted stance with good structure. Your right forearm is naturally bent and relaxed and intercepts the Wooden-Man's active middle arm. Your left arm is also naturally bent and relaxed and intercepts the Wooden-Man's right arm in the high gate area.

**6th Move:** Shift to center by taking left hand drive down the body to a groin tear—using your back knuckles to intercept the groin. Tear downward. Left shoulder should contract to intercept the Wooden-Man's right arm. The back hand of your right hand intercepts the Wooden-Man's left arm. Your left knee does knee destruction on the Wooden-Man very quickly. Make sure that your left foot is turned into the Wooden-Man's leg line. It is very important that you hit his knee with the top of your knee to insure you do not do damage to your own knee.

**7th Move:** Your right leg shifts right and pulls your left leg to a 50-50 weight ratio. Your left hand comes up from groin to a forearm control underneath the Wooden-Man's left arm. Your right hand intercepts Wooden-Man's left arm—palm facing toward the right side of the Wooden-Man. Your left forearm pulls your body to the left side of the Wooden-Man as that move frees up your right hand to strike his face bag in a blood pulse, palm facing you. Make contact while palm rolls outward. Your left leg springs up to a downward thrust to the Wooden-Man's active leg at the knee joint. Or a heel hook to the inside of the knee joint can also be undertaken.

**8th Move:** Start with left leg. Shift left leg back to center and pull right leg to the right side of the Wooden-Man's active leg. Your right arm extends naturally to intercept left arm of the Wooden-Man as a high gate strike. Your left arm intercepts the Wooden-Man's low active arm as a natural extension to block a middle gate attack.

**9th Move:** Your left forearm rolls up to intercept active right arm of the Wooden-Man on a high gate attack while your right arm circles underneath to strike face bag. Feet are 50-50 as your left leg is placed on the left side of the Wooden-Man's active leg. Your right leg is to the right side of the active leg of the Wooden-Man. Your left foot is lead.

**10th Move:** Your leg position stays the same as it does in Move 9. Your left hand rolls over in a tiger claw, pulling the body forward while the right hand explodes into a fist strike to the face bag.

**11<sup>th</sup> Move:** Shift your weight left while keeping the foot position the same. Your left hand rolls over the top to the outside of the Wooden-Man's right arm, in a Tiger Claw position. I want you to feel like your pulling meat off the bone. Your right hand does a Tiger Claw to the inside of the Wooden-Man's left arm.

**12th Move:** Shift your weight back to center, again in a 50-50 ratio. Raise your left hand to an open Tiger Claw to the face bag. Use your 3rd arm (left shoulder) to guide Wooden-Man's right arm. Right hand checks left arm of the Wooden-Man while also in a Tiger Claw position.

**13th Move:** Your left hand picks up the right active arm of the Wooden-Man in a Tiger Claw position. Your fingers face towards you. Your right hand stops right active arm from moving. Your left arm expands and breaks the Wooden-Man's right active arm as a spring in a trap.

**14th Move:** Your left hand goes under the Wooden-Man's right arm and pulls your body to the left side of the Wooden-Man. Your left hand openly intercepts left arm of the Wooden-Man while right hand explodes in a Tiger Claw to the face bag. Spring forth your left leg to a knee stomp or a heel hook.

**15th Move:** Pull your left leg back to center and both feet shift to a 50-50 weight ratio. Your right hand is extended naturally to cover and block left arm of the Wooden-Man. Your left arm naturally bends as your left hand drops over the Wooden-Man's middle active arm.

**16th Move:** Pivot left (Move on the balls of your feet and shift on your heels—still in a 50-50 weight ration). Your left hand, which is on the inside, rises to intercept the Wooden-Man's right arm. Drop your right hand down the center line to strike the groin bag in a tear like motion. Using your back hand knuckles, drive downward. Your right knee thrusts into the Wooden-Man's active leg at the knee joint. Make sure you turn your right foot to face the target as in Move 3.

**17ᵗʰ Move:** Lively step left while pulling right leg to a 50-50 weight stance. You should be on the right side of the Wooden-Man's body. Your right forearm rises to intercept Wooden-Man's right arm in a lifting motion. Your left hand does a Monkey slap block to the Wooden-Man's right arm allowing you to hook and pull with your right hand, which in turn frees up your left hand. Your left hand hits in a cutting motion with fingers rising to the face bag. When you hit the face bag, open your fingers and let the energy transfer through to the face bag. This will do more damage than closing your fingers. Your right leg springs up to a foot stomp to the Wooden-Man's active leg at the knee joint. Or, execute a heel hook to the same location.

**18th Move:** Your right foot pulls back to center. Drag left foot to a 50-50 weight stance. Your left foot is lead. Your right arm is relaxed and extended to intercept the Wooden-Man's active middle arm. Your left arm is also relaxed and extended to intercept the Wooden-Man's right active arm.

**19th Move:** Your foot position stays the same. Your left hand is raised—palm facing outward. Do a Monkey slap block downward through the Wooden-Man's active right arm, while right hand also rises with a Monkey slap to block in an upward motion the Wooden-Man's active left arm.

**20th Move:** Your foot position stays the same. Left leg leads. Remember always to stand in a natural stance. That way you can attack or defend with either leg as it is faster. Your right arm rises and the wrist flips hand over Wooden-Man's active left arm, like a trap motion. Your left arm moves downward to strike at the rib line making sure you split the rope in simulating splitting ribs. This will make it harder for your opponent to breath. Therefore the victory is yours.

**21st Move:** Lean right while still in a 50-50 weight stance. As your right hand is in a Tiger claw, do a Monkey slap with your right hand. Hit the nerve on the inside of forearm at the elbow joint with the right hand. Your left hand goes into a guard position on the center line, about five to six inches from your chest cavity.

**22ⁿᵈ Move:** Shift left. Your left leg is lead and you're still in a 50-50 weight stance. Your left hand does a Monkey slap with Tiger claw on Wooden-Man's left arm. Make sure the thumb of your left hand does a nerve strike at the elbow joint of the Wooden-Man. Your right hand covers the center line about five to six inches from your chest cavity.

**23rd Move:** Repeat move 21.

**24th Move:** Take live step to the left. Pull your right leg as to a 50-50 stance. You should be on the right side of the Wooden-Man. Your right hand traps extended right active arm at the end while simultaneously your left palm rises to break Wooden-Man's active right arm.

**25th Move:** Maintain left position. Your right hand rolls over to guide active right arm of the Wooden-Man. Your right hand does a knife strike to the face bag. Your fingers face upward—in a relaxed mode to allow all the energy to transfer from you to the face bag. This will increase the damage done to your attacker.

**26th Move:** Execute a live step with your right foot and pull left foot to a 50-50 weighted stance. Now you are in the center of the Wooden-Man. Your left hand flips over the Wooden-Man's active right arm as in a pulling and striping motion. Your right hand explodes into a fist to strike stomach area in the middle gate—right below the rib line.

**27th Move:** Shift to the right. You are now attacking the left side of the Wooden-Man in a rolling stripping motion. Your left arm is bent with palm to the outside of the right shoulder. Your right arm is extended. (Remember to try to be as natural as possible.) Do not lock your elbow joint. This extends to the arm pit of the Wooden-Man. This motion will do a forearm, elbow and shoulder lock all at the same time.

**28th Move:** Your hands coil like a snake. Absorb and draw back in a spring like motion. Prepare for a double strike to both high and middle gate. Your right hand is in a high gate attack mode while left hand attacks the middle gate area. Your left leg takes a live step in toward the Wooden-Man's body. You are now on the left side of the Wooden-Man.

**29th Move:** Take live step toward the Wooden-Man. Execute a right hand to the face bag. Simultaneously hit the groin bag with your left hand. Your hands are in a Tiger claw position. Your hands should hit, grab and pull. Feel the rocks in the bag as they separate as you are simulating the tearing of soft tissue.

**30<sup>th</sup> Move:** Your left leg shoots back to center—in a live step. Pull your right leg in to a 50-50 weight stance. Your right and left hands circle around to intercept Wooden-Man's active left and right arms respectively—your right intercepts left active arm and your left intercepts right active arm in a circling motion. This is done at the end of the Wooden-Man's arm joints. Make sure you lift the extended arms up. This will expose or open up the middle gate area for a middle gate attack.

**31st Move:** The right side of your body turns toward the center of the Wooden-Man. Trap the middle gate, active arm with your left hand in a Tiger claw position. Your right forearm breaks the middle active arm with your right arm in a natural bent and relaxed position. Your thumb is facing your Don Tein at the center of your body.

**32$^{nd}$ Move:** Shift left while trapping extended right active arm with your left hand. Shoot underneath active arm and grab the arm pit with your right hand in a Tiger claw motion. Remember to hit, grab and pull.

**33rd Move:** This move simulates a monkey. Your left hand covers the back of your head in a circular motion. Your whole body then folds at qua or center. Spring forward with your right foot to a thrust kick to the rib line in the middle gate area. Your left leg is a rooted base. Your right hand is on the inside of the Wooden-Man's active arm and acts as a guide, which will create an opening to strike the face bag with your left hand in a Tiger claw position. Remember to hit, grab and pull.

**34th Move:** Your right leg shifts back to center pulling left leg to a 50-50 weight stance. Your left side is lead. Your left arm intercepts the middle active arm of the Wooden-Man with your palm facing downward. Your right hand is in a pre-block position and is five to six inches from your chest cavity.

**35th Move:** Shoot your left arm underneath Wooden-Man's active left arm and pull your body to the left side of the Wooden-Man, while maintaining contact with your right hand. This will trap and break the left active arm of the Wooden-Man. Your left leg is lead.

**36th Move:** Position yourself all the way to the right. Attack the left side of the Wooden-Man. This is a Monkey. It is the same move as in #33. However, the attack is on the Wooden-Man's left side this time. Your right hand circles over your head, while at the same time your left hand intercepts Wooden-Man's active left arm. Your left foot does a thrust kick to the rib line in the middle gate area. Bend at the qua or center. Your right leg is a rooted base. Crouch like a monkey and strike like a monkey.

**37th Move:** Your left leg does a live step to center of Wooden-Man, while pulling right leg to a 50-50 weight stance. Remember, if you are not in a natural fighting stance, you are going to be slow to respond to an attack. Your left arm bends naturally and intercepts middle active arm. Your right arm is also bent naturally and intercepts Wooden-Man's active left arm.

**38th Move:** Stay in center of the Wooden-Man. Your left side is lead. Intercept Wooden-Man's active right arm with your left forearm. Begin to roll your left hand in a Tiger claw position. Your right hand curls into a fist and prepares to strike the high gate area.

**39th Move:** Stay in center. Your left foot is still lead and in a 50-50 weight stance. Now you are in a right side lead, with left hand in Tiger claw position. Your left hand makes contact and simulates stripping the blood from the Wooden-Man's right active arm. This will make the limb weak. At the same time, strike the face bag with your right fist. Make sure your hand is vertical and your elbow is down. Remember never to fully extend or to lock out. This is unnatural and can cause damage to you.

**40th Move:** Rock back and pull your body. Your left leg is lead. Collapse both of your arms around the outside of the Wooden-Man's active right and active left arms in the high gate area. Your arms are extended (but not fully) and palms facing upward. Your inside elbows should make contact with the Wooden-Man's active arms at the elbow joints. This move draws your opponent in.

**41st Move:** Remain in a left leg lead while both right and left hands drop over the top of the Wooden-Man's active arms in the high gate area, on the inside of the active arms. This move guides the Wooden-Man's active right and left arms to the outside. This, in turn, creates an energy hole in the middle gate area at the rib line. Draw in for your next attack. An energy hole is a strategic place on the body of the Wooden-Man or any opponent; and is a created opening for your next attack.

**42nd Move:** Remain in left leg lead. Rock back and roll your hands over the Wooden-Man's active right and left arms to simulate a snake head when it turns. Use double Tiger clawed hands to attack the rib line in the middle gate area. Shoot in and execute splitting of ribs. Both your hands strike at the same time in the middle gate region. Splitting the ribs will make it hard for the attacker to breath.

**43rd Move:** Remain in the left leg lead. Both your arms come up to intercept Wooden-Man's active right and left arms in the high gate area. As your arms are on the inside, guide the Wooden-Man's active arms to the outside thus creating a strategic opening for your next attack.

**44th Move:** Remain in left leg lead. Shoot up from center on both active right and left arms on the inside. Place both your hands in a Tiger claw position and explode to the face bag, striking with your thumbs. Shoot your thumbs to the eye sockets and temporarily blind your attacker.

**45th Move:** Repeat move 40.

**46th Move:** Simultaneously move both hands. Shift right while still in a 50-50 weight stance. Your right hand flips and drops over the left active arm of the Wooden-Man in an upward motion. Your left hand circles and flips over the right active arm in a downward motion. Your right hand goes up as your left hand goes down. Remember the circles. This is a snake coiling around its prey.

**47th Move:** Simultaneously move both of your hands. Shift left while still in a 50-50 weight stance. Your right hand goes in a downward motion and circles over left active arm of the Wooden-Man. Your left hand goes upward in a circular motion. Remember your right hand is on the inside of the Wooden-Man's active left arm and your left hand is on the outside of the Wooden-Man's active right arm. Your right hand goes down as your left hand goes up.

**48th Move:** Repeat move 46.

**49th Move:** Shift left and take a live step with your left leg. Pull right leg to a 50-50 weighted stance. Your right hand shoots underneath active right arm of the Wooden-Man. Use Tiger hand claw to hit, grab and pull arm pit. Your left hand traps the right active arm on the outside so you can either break right arm or do a joint lock.

**50th Move:** Your body position shoots left. At the same time, your right hand hooks over and pulls active right arm of the Wooden-Man. This will free up your left hand to do a Tiger claw hit to the face bag. Again, hit, grab and pull. Spring your right foot to do a foot stomp on the Wooden-Man's active right leg at the knee joint area or apply a heel hook to the same location. Your whole body position is on the right side of the Wooden-Man.

**51st Move:** Live step with right foot to the center of the Wooden-Man in a shoot like motion. Pull left foot to center location. Your left foot is lead. Your arms are relaxed and extended. Your right arm intercepts the middle active arm of the Wooden-Man on the inside of the limb. Your left arm intercepts active right arm on the outside and in the high gate area of the Wooden-Man.

**52nd Move:** Gain some distance from the Wooden-Man by shooting your right foot back while still on center. Your left leg is lead. Do a re-direction of energy by doing Monkey slaps to the extended arms of the Wooden-Man with your right hand going up as your left hand goes down. Do this at the end of the limbs of the Wooden-Man in the high gate area.

**53rd Move:** Shoot toward the Wooden-Man while staying in center. Your left leg is still lead. Close the distance between you and the Wooden-Man while using Monkey slaps. Now your right hand goes down at the end of the limb as your left hand goes up at the end of the limb in the high gate area.

**54th Move:** Repeat move 52.

**55th Move:** Spring forward. Your left foot is still lead. Your left hand flips over and traps the Wooden-Man's active left arm on the inside. Shoot left hand in a Tiger claw motion at the middle gate of the Wooden-Man in the rib line area. Make sure to split the rope to simulate splitting the ribs or compressing the chest cavity of the Wooden-Man.

**56th Move:** Now do drunken stepping. Your right foot takes a quarter step back. Pull your left foot back to a 50-50 weight stance. Shoot your right foot forward to the left side of the Wooden-Man while pulling left foot to a position at the weight stance of 50-50. It is a four count. When you do it fast, you fall toward the corner where you let your feet pick up underneath and re-stabilize. Your right foot is now leading. Your left hand shoots underneath Wooden-Man's active left arm in the middle gate area and strikes the arm pit in a Tiger claw position. Hit, grab and pull. Your right hand traps the active left arm of the Wooden-Man as it is on the inside of the active left arm in the high gate area.

**57th Move:** Your right foot is lead. Pull your left hand in a Tiger claw hand position and grab at the elbow joint. This will free up your right hand to do a Tiger claw hand strike to the face bag. Hit, grab and pull. You are now on the left side of the Wooden-Man. Your left foot springs upward to do a stomp to the knee joint of the active leg of the Wooden-Man or apply a heel hook to the inside of the knee joint area.

**58th Move:** Your left foot shoots back to center. Your right leg is still lead. Your body position is facing the Wooden-Man in the center. Your right forearm is placed at the elbow joint of the Wooden-Man's active left arm in the high gate area. Your left forearm intercepts the middle active arm in the middle gate and is placed on the outside of the limb. Both your right and left arms are relaxed and extended. Your arms position placement is at the elbow joint in both high and middle gate.

**59th Move:** Now, facing center of the Wooden-Man with your right leg as lead, your left forearm raises in a Monkey block. Then your left hand rolls from palm facing you to your palm turned away in an upward motion. Your right hand curls into a fist on center line and prepares to crush the face bag in the high gate area.

**60th Move:** Your right leg is still lead and you're still in a 50-50 weight stance. Explode right fist to face bag. Remember, once you make contact, open your hand a little and let all the energy transfer to the face bag. A tightly closed fist is like a dam stopping energy from flowing through to the target area. Your left hand does a Tiger claw grab to the Wooden-Man's active right arm at the elbow joint. Do a slight pull to accelerate the face bag in a collision with your right fist.

**61st Move:** Left leg is lead. Your hands are like snake heads searching for its next meal. Use your fingers as a snake tongue. Feel the heart beat of your prey. When you strike, open your hands as a snake would when it bites. Shift right and strike the right active arm in the high gate. Use your right Snake hand and attack the Wooden-Man at the elbow joint. Remember to uncoil and let the energy flow. Your left hand is in a pre-block mode—five to six inches from your chest cavity on center line.

**62nd Move:** Still in a snake position, lift your right foot a quarter step and pull left foot to a 50-50 weight position. Shift your body left, while still in center. Attack left active arm of the Wooden-Man at the elbow joint in the high gate. Still using your right Snake hand, open your thumb of your right hand in a snake head fashion and bite the nerves in the Wooden-Man's active left arm. Then, roll over the top of the active left arm and uncoil the snake's body. Make sure you trap the active left arm with your left hand—as you want to hold your prey.

**63rd Move:** Repeat move 61.

**64th Move:** This move shifts from Snake to Tiger. Shift left. Your right hand goes from Snake to Tiger while rolling over the top of the Wooden-Man's active right arm in the high gate—in a trap like motion. You are now on the right side of the Wooden-Man. At the same time, your left hand circles around in a Tiger hand fashion to split the rope of the Wooden-Man in the middle gate as in simulating splitting the ribs. Remember to hit, grab and pull.

**65$^{Th}$ Move:** Shoot back with right foot to the center of the Wooden-Man. Pull left foot forward as left foot is now lead. Settle when you reach 50-50 weight stance. Your body is in the center of the Wooden-Man. Your right forearm intercepts the Wooden-Man's active left arm at the elbow joint in the high gate. Right forearm is extended and naturally bent. Your right arm is on the inside of the active left arm. Draw back and pull—think Tiger! Your left forearm is extended and naturally bent and guides the middle active arm of the Wooden-Man at the elbow joint. Your left forearm is on the inside of the middle active arm in the middle gate.

**66th Move:** Shoot in as your left leg is lead. Your right hand explodes to the face bag in a Tiger Claw position in the high gate. Remember to hit, grab and pull. Your left hand shoots in to the rib line area, which is also in a Tiger claw position at the middle gate.

**67th Move:** Shift right while your left hand shoots underneath active left arm in the high gate of the Wooden-Man in a saw like cutting motion. Your right hand traps the left active arm in the same location on the inside of the limb while being relaxed and naturally bent. This will either break the active left arm of the Wooden-Man or it will destroy the soft tissue of the active limb of your attacker.

**68th Move:** Use your left hand to pull your body to the right. Coil like a snake and prepare to strike with both hands in the high and middle gate areas. Your left hand is targeting the face bag and your right hand is targeting the groin bag. Your left forearm maintains contact with the left active arm of the Wooden-Man so that your senses will connect with your opponent and relay its motion to you before it happens.

**69th Move:** Advance towards the Wooden-Man's body and close gap. Your right foot is lead. Uncoil your body to strike the Wooden-Man. Your left hand moves to the face bag in a Tiger claw position in the high gate. Your right hand goes to the groin bag also in a Tiger claw position in the middle gate. Remember to hit, grab and pull. Feel the rocks or iron in the bags separate as you simulate destroying soft tissue.

**70th Move:** Live step back with left leg. Your right leg is lead. Advance your right arm underneath active left arm of the Wooden-Man in the high gate area—using a downward cutting motion. Trap the left active arm with the back of your left hand in same location. Remember your hands act like scissors when cutting paper. This will simulate destroying soft tissue of which the Wooden-Man represents and also that of a tiger taking the limb of its prey for better tactical advantage.

**71st Move:** Advance toward center with right foot as lead. Double Tiger claw to the middle gate. You want to attack both sides of the rib line at the same time. Use your thumbs to split the rope of the Wooden-Man.

**72nd Move:** Shift left so you are on the right side of the Wooden-Man. Use live stepping to shift lead foot position. Your left foot is in the lead now. Your right forearm shoots underneath the Wooden-Man's active right arm as your left hand traps in a scissors like motion to simulate cutting soft tissue. Your left hand is on the inside of the Wooden-Man's active right arm.

**73rd Move:** Advance in with right foot and pull your body till you reach a 50-50 weight stance. Use double Tiger hand strike in the middle gate region at the rib line. Remember to split the rope in the middle gate area as you would normally split the ribs of your attacker. Both hands strike at the same time. You are now on the right side of the Wooden-Man.

**74th Move:** Draw right foot back to center. Your left foot is lead now. Your right hand folds over active middle arm in the middle gate. Your left forearm intercepts right active arm of the Wooden-Man in the high gate.

**75th Move:** Your left foot is lead. In one motion, move both of your hands at the same time in a Monkey hand slap fashion. Your right hand goes up on the left active arm of the Wooden-Man and your left hand goes down on the right active arm of the Wooden-Man. This is done on the elbow joint of both right and left active arms in the high gate area. Also, this move will split the attention of your attacker and give you a strategic opening for your next attack.

**76th Move:** Remain with left foot lead. Your right hand drops over the left active arm in the high gate. Simultaneously, your left hand, which is in a Tiger claw position, strikes the rib line on the right side of the Wooden-Man in the middle gate area. Make sure you use the thumb of your left hand to split the rope. Remember you are simulating splitting the ribs of your attacker. This will make it very difficult for your attacker to breath. This move will give you time to flee to safety.

**77th Move:** Do drunken stepping to switch your foot position from a left leg lead to a right leg lead. Settle to root before you strike. Your right hand does a Tiger claw and pulls the meat from the bone, in simulation, of the Wooden-Man's left arm in the high gate. Simultaneously, your left hand, which is also in a Tiger claw position, strips the flesh off the Wooden-Man's middle active arm in the middle gate. Think Tiger. Remember, you want to punish the attacker's limbs so that either he or she will never want to strike you again.

**78ᵗʰ Move:** Do drunken stepping to switch from a right leg lead back to a left leg lead. Your left hand remains in a Tiger claw position and attacks the outside of the Wooden-Man's active right arm in the high gate area. Your motion is to grab and tear. Your hands will operate as in wind shield wipers covering 180 degree half circle—in a Tiger hand claw formation. Your right hand—also in a Tiger claw position, tears flesh from the Wooden-Man's active middle arm in the middle gate on the inside of the limb.

**79th Move:** Repeat move 77.

**80th Move:** Shift left as your right hand shoots underneath the Wooden-Man's active right arm in the high gate and executes a sawing like cutting motion. The target is the arm pit. Hit, grab and pull. Your left hand traps the extended right arm of the Wooden-Man at the same location on the outside of the extended limb in the high gate. Remember to do a scissors like motion. This action done on the Wooden-Man will simulate separating soft tissue from the bone on your attacker's body.

**81ˢᵗ Move:** Shift all the way left so you are on the right side of the Wooden-Man's body. Your right hand goes from the arm pit to a Tiger claw grab on the extended right active arm at the elbow joint in the high gate. Your left hand is free to do a Tiger claw strike to the face bag also in the high gate. Execute a hit, grab and pull. Your left leg is the rooted base while the right foot does a knee stomp. Or apply a heel hook to the inside of the active leg in the knee joint area of the Wooden-Man in the low gate. Remember to make contact and drive downward or hook across the knee joint to ensure maximum damage to the active leg.

**82nd Move:** Trap active right arm with your right hand and do a joint lock with your body. You need to roll over the top of the right active arm of the Wooden-Man with your left arm. Extend and execute an attack to the active left arm at the end of the limb in the high gate. The fingers of your left hand face away from the Wooden-Man's body. Your right hand holds active right arm and left hand attacks active left arm in a Tiger claw hand formation. In simulation, this action will break the right active arm.

**83rd Move:** Use your left hand in a Tiger claw position and allow yourself to be pulled across the Wooden-Man's body—you are now on the left side. Your left hand rolls over and guides active left arm on the outside. Simultaneously, shoot your right hand—in a Tiger claw formation, and press the eye sockets of the face bag of the Wooden-Man. This action simulates your attacker being temporally blinded and gives you time and the advantage of getting away.

**84th Move:** Shift back to center. Stand neutral while facing the Wooden-Man's body while still in a 50-50 weight stance. This is a Close Horse stance—knees slightly bent and settled while maintaining root before you strike using Tiger claw. Your left hand explodes to the face bag, while your right hand drops over and hooks the active left arm of the Wooden-Man. Use the paws of the tiger in a circular motion and claw at the Wooden-Man's face bag. In simulation, this move will also do damage to the eye sockets and temporally decreases the vision of your opponent thus giving you the opportunity and time to get away to safety.

**85th Move:** Shift leg and trap extended right active arm of the Wooden-Man with the back of your left hand while you do a saw like cutting motion with your right forearm. Pull yourself to the right side of the Wooden-Man's body. In simulation, this move will attack the soft tissue of the extended active right arm in the high gate.

**86th Move:** You shift all the way left so you are on the right side of the Wooden-Man. Your left leg is lead. In a Tiger claw position, your right hand rolls over grabs and pulls the Wooden-Man's active right arm. Simultaneously, you strike with your left hand, which is also in a Tiger claw position. Your goal is to strike the rib line in the middle gate area. Remember to split the rope.

**87th Move:** Repeat move 82.

**88th Move:** Pull yourself across the body of the Wooden-Man. You are now on the left side of the Wooden-Man. Your left hand flips over the active left arm in the high gate and guides the limb. Your right hand explodes to the face bag and squishes the eye socket to temporarily blind the Wooden-Man or in simulation, your attacker. This move will create an opening for you to flee.

**89th Move:** Shoot right leg back till you reach a 50-50 weight stance. Your left leg is lead. Intercept left upper gate and middle gate active arms of the Wooden-Man. Your right arm guides left active arm as your left hand folds over to guide active middle arm.

**90th Move:** Left foot is in lead position. Roll left forearm underneath the Wooden-Man's active right arm in the high gate with palm facing you. Turn palm away from you in order to create an opening to the face bag. Get ready to explode your right fist—to crush the rock or iron in the face bag in the high gate of the Wooden-Man.

**91ˢᵗ Move:** Your foot position stays the same. In Tiger claw formation, your left hand pulls right active arm at the elbow joint to cause an explosive collision with your right fist and the face bag of the Wooden-Man in the high gate.

**92$^{nd}$ Move:** Your right hand circles around the active left arm in the high gate of the Wooden-Man to strike the middle gate active arm. Simultaneously, your left hand—in a Monkey position, traps and holds active middle arm so as not to let it move. This action will break the middle arm in the middle gate. Spring forward with your right hand in Tiger claw position to strike the groin bag. Remember to hit, grab and pull. Your right knee does a Thrusting Pulse to the active leg on the knee joint of the Wooden-Man. Make sure your right foot is turned toward the targeted area. This will insure that you do not do damage to your own knee.

**93ʳᵈ Move:** Switch positions and keep low as a monkey would when it strikes. Trap active middle arm with your right hand. In a Tiger claw position, spring forth your left hand to strike the groin bag. Remember to hit, grab and pull. Now your left knee does a Knee Pulse to the active leg of the Wooden-Man in the knee joint area. Remember, turn your foot to face the targeted area as this will insure you do not damage to your own knee.

**94th Move:** Repeat move 92.

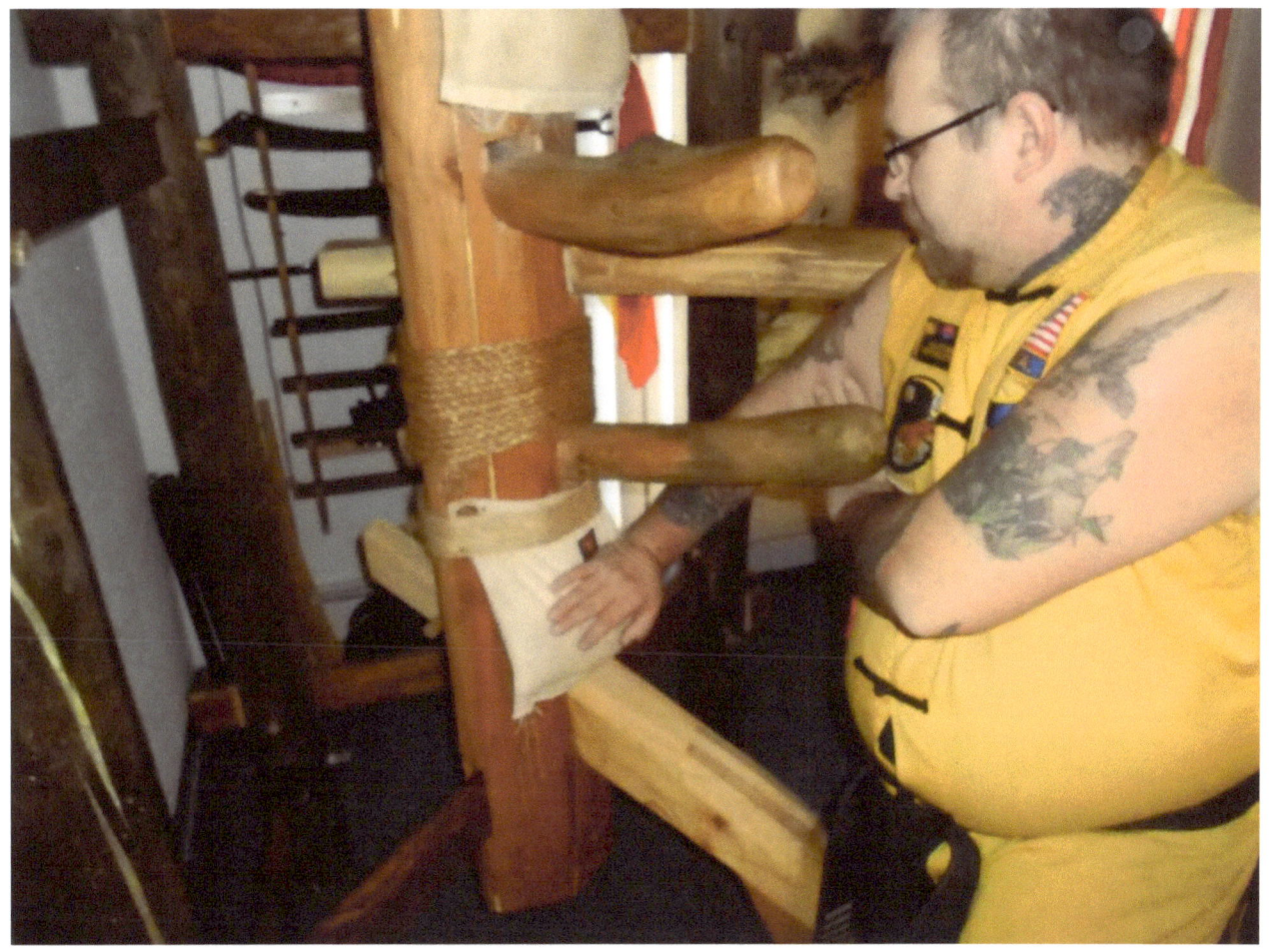

**95th Move:** Like a snake, uncoil and spring up from the Monkey position. Both hands simultaneously strike the Wooden-Man's active left arm in the high gate. Both of your hands are in a Tiger claw formation. Your left hand is above the elbow joint on the inside of the limb and your right hand is also on the inside of the limb, but below the elbow joint.

**96th Move:** Repeat move 93.

**97th Move:** Moves 92, 94 and 97 are the same. Remember to strike like a monkey and stay low.

**98th Move:** Repeat moves 93, 96 and 98. They are the same. Again, stay low and strike like a monkey.

**99th Move:** Uncoil like a snake and spring up from the monkey position. Simultaneously, both of your hands strike the Wooden-Man's active right arm with both hands in a Tiger claw formation. Your right hand is above the elbow joint and your left hand is below the elbow joint. Both hands are attacking on the inside of the limb and in the high gate area.

**100th Move:** Shoot left so that you are on the right side of the Wooden-Man. Your right hand flips over the active right arm in the high gate and grabs the limb in a Tiger claw hand formation. Pull the arm of the Wooden-Man's body toward you. Get ready for a low gate attack with your right foot at the Wooden-Man's core center in the low gate area. This move attacks the base or rooted leg.

**101st Move:** In a Tiger claw formation, your right hand grabs and holds the right active arm in the high gate. Execute a slight pull to cause a mind split from high to low gate, which is where you are attacking now. Thrust your right foot forward to a low gate attack to the Wooden-Man's body base. This move simulates taking out the rooted or base leg of your attacker. Your left hand stays on a pre-block mode that is five to six inches from your chest cavity.

**102ⁿᵈ Move:** You remain rooted and based with your left leg. Thrust your right foot to attack the knee joint of the Wooden-Man in the low gate. Continue contact with your right Tiger claw on the active arm of the Wooden-Man in the high gate. On this strike, you want to pull the right active arm of the Wooden-Man as you kick the leg. This move will split the mind of the attacker and he or she will not know where the next strike will come from. Your left hand is in a pre-block motion that is five to six inches from your chest cavity thus guarding your middle and high gate areas.

**103rd Move:** Remain rooted and based with your left leg. Tiger claw hand maintains a grab of the right active arm of the Wooden-Man in a pulling motion. Thrust your right lead foot and execute a kick to the ankle area in the low gate while maintaining a pre-block with your left hand on center line.

**104th Move:** Shoot to the middle of the Wooden-Man. Your left forearm intercepts middle active arm in the middle gate. Your right hand is in a pre-block mode at the center of the body line—five to six inches from your chest cavity.

**105th Move:** Move all the way to the right so as to place you on the left side of the Wooden-Man's body. Your left arm is extended and making contact with the active left arm of the Wooden-Man at the elbow joint in the high gate. Your right hand is in a pre-block mode to cover any middle or high gate attacks. Your left foot is lead.

**106th Move:** Use your left hand in a Tiger claw position to pull your Wooden-Man's left active arm in the high gate area. This move will split the mind of your attacker and he or she will not be able to tell where the next strike is coming from. Execute the high gate pull on the left active arm when you do a thrust kick to the low gate. Strike with your left foot to the body's base in a thrust like kicking motion in the low gate. Your right leg is rooted and acts like your base as this will stabilize you for your low line attacks. Your right hand is in a pre-block mode to cover middle and high gate advancements.

**107th Move:** Maintain right hand in a pre-block mode. Your left hand remains in a Tiger claw formation on the left active arm of the Wooden-Man in the high gate. However, before you execute a thrusting kick to the low gate area, you must give a little pull to the left active arm in the high gate. Again, this will cause confusion in the mind of your attacker. Execute a thrusting kick with your left foot. Following, your left foot does a stomp to the knee joint area. Your right leg will stabilize you as it is your rooted base.

**108th Move:** Your right hand remains in a pre-block mode to cover middle and high gate attacks. Your left hand remains in a Tiger claw formation on the active left arm in the high gate. Same as before, you want to do a slight pull on the left active arm so you can split the mind of your attacker. Your left lead foot executes a stomp to the ankle area of the active leg in the low gate.

**109th Move:** Shift back to center. Your feet are in a neutral 50-50 weight stance. This is a relaxed Horse posture. Your right arm is naturally bent and extended to intercept the Wooden-Man's active left arm in the high gate. Your left arm is also naturally bent and extended to intercept active middle arm in the middle gate.

**110th Move:** Shift weight back and attack the active right arm in the high gate with a low saw like cutting motion with your right forearm. Your left back hand traps active right arm and acts like a scissors so as to allow the right forearm to do the cutting. In simulation, this action will disturb and/or destroy soft tissue of the Wooden-Man's extended right arm.

**111th Move:** Continue shifting left so your whole body is on the right side of the Wooden-Man. Use a Tiger claw hand position to attack and grab the right active arm with your left hand. Do not let the limb go. Your right hand grabs wrist to forearm and does a shearing like cutting motion to break the right active limb in the high gate. Simultaneously, shoot your right foot in a stomping motion to the active leg of the Wooden-Man. Your left leg acts as a rooted base to allow you structure and stability so that you can strike in multiples of three.

**112th Move:** Shoot with right foot to the center of the Wooden-Man and follow up with your left foot till you reach a 50-50 weight stance. Continue to execute a low block to the middle active arm with your left forearm. Your right hand remains in a pre-block mode on center line. Remember to move like a monkey throughout the body of the Wooden-Man.

**113th Move:** Shift right to do a downward angle strike to the active left arm of the Wooden-Man with your left forearm. Your right hand is in a pre-block mode on center line. Your stance is springy and fast to respond to an attack—think like a monkey.

**114th Move:** Pull yourself all the way to the right so you are on the left side of the Wooden-Man. Your right hand is in a Tiger claw position—pulling and grabbing left active arm above the elbow joint. Simultaneously, your left hand in a Tiger claw position grabs left active arm below the elbow joint and does a shear like breaking motion. At the same time, spring up your left foot to do a knee stomp on the active leg of the Wooden-Man. Your right leg is a structured rooted base that allows you to strike in a three count—both low and high gate, at the same time.

**115th Move:** Shoot back to center with left foot in lead position. Your right arm is naturally bent, relaxed and extended to intercept an oncoming attack from the high gate area of the Wooden-Man's left active arm. Your left arm is also naturally bent and relaxed and is extended to intercept an attack from the middle active arm in the middle gate region.

**116th Move:** Remain in the center line of the Wooden-Man. Your left foot is in lead position. Raise your left forearm with palm facing you to your palm turned away from you in a 180 degree turn. Raise and block the right active arm of the Wooden-Man in the high gate. This action will cause a diversion. Prepare to strike the face bag with your left fist.

**117th Move:** Your body position stays the same as it did in move 116. You follow through with your exploding right fist to the face bag and crush the rock or iron.

**118th Move:** After you strike the face bag, collapse both your right and left arms to the outside of the Wooden-Man's active right and left arms in the high gate. Do this in a relaxed manner. Your right forearm intercepts the left active arm of the Wooden-Man and your left forearm intercepts the right active arm in the high gate region. Remember, tension stops energy flow. Your feet position is in a close Horse stance—naturally bent and relaxed. Your weight position is 50-50.

**119th Move:** Draw back from center to gain some distance between you and the Wooden-Man. Both of your hands simultaneously draw back from both active right and left arms in the high gate region. Your right forearm is on the left active arm and your left forearm is on the right active arm. Both of your hands are on the inside in a pulling like motion. Think Tiger!

**120th Move:** Pounce like a hungry tiger to its kill. Spring forward with a double Tiger hand claw to the middle region and strike simultaneously with both right and left Tiger hands. Attack both sides of the simulated rib cage at the same time and enjoy the attack.

**Close:** Take three steps back—starting with your left foot. Close with a humble Buddhist bow. Remember to thank the Wooden-Man and the animal sets for all the knowledge that they have transferred to you.

# Fighting and Training History

    My training began at the young age of nine. I trained in a karate style called Kempo. That got my taste buds craving for combat, although I had a huge respect for my fellow human beings. I was a troubled youth and had a lot of family problems. I turned to the street for guidance. Then I turned to drugs and alcohol. I was placed in foster care and shelter homes. My first drug and alcohol treatment was when I was at the age of fourteen. Following that, I got into trouble with the law when I was arrested for felony possession and selling of fire arms across state lines. It was in this period that found me in my first gang fight with knives. There were three of us and ten of them—all of which survived. However, stemming from that fight, I ended up in a psychiatric hospital on Halloween night. Following, I was placed in a group home where I stayed for a year and a half.

    My foster dad was in the Marines and he did two tours in Vietnam in Charley Company. I loved it when he showed me combative moves and tell me stories on how he survived the war. I had an offer to go to South America and be trained as a mercenary for hire to be engaged in the drug wars. That experience landed me back in jail at the age of seventeen where I stayed until I tried to break out. It was in this period that I had an offer to help a family whose daughters were raped. I was asked to take out the perpetrator who did this horrible crime. The situation got me three felonies in the county jail. There they placed me in Maximum Security at the age of eighteen where I stayed for two years and fought along-side the Cubans. I survived it and was released. Then I said to myself that I would never survive another stint in prison.

    I thought the one and only thing I was good at was fighting. So, I decided that I would continue my training on how to be a better fighter. I discovered the Chuan-Lu organization offering martial arts. They took me under their wing and gave me guidance. While in this training, I became proficient in the fighting arts and learned how to become a better person. Through this, I became at peace with myself. I would take jobs in security such as the head bouncer at a local bar in Hudson, Wisconsin. I also did MOSH pit security for both the EDGE Fest and the

OZ Fest along with security at WEE Fest. I learned how to take control over someone without hurting that individual. I continued on with my studies and started teaching martial arts. In Hudson, I founded the Loa-Hu Kung-Fu fighting system.

      During a stint in New Mexico, I taught Kung Fu at the Eastern New Mexico University while also teaching Kung-Fu at a public school in Ruidoso on Main Street. I continued teaching while I lived there. Then I moved back to the Wisconsin area. Once returned, I focused on iron palm training and breaking concrete blocks—bare handed. I also continued my training with the Grand Master of the Chuan Lu organization of martial arts in Chi Gung. I learned how to transfer energy throughout my body and be able to transmit this energy to other fellow human beings for healing purposes. Presently, I continue to teach in the Hudson, Wisconsin area. I have developed my own style called Loa-Hu Kung-Fu, which means Tiger's way or in other words, the way of the tiger. I hope you will not have to go through what I did in order to accomplish your goals. I can offer real life combat situations and show you how to do this without risk to your person. I hope this book will help you in your martial arts experience.

                              Grand Master, Tim M. Armstrong

# The End.

www.ingramcontent.com/pod-product-compliance
Lightning Source LLC
Chambersburg PA
CBHW041703160426
43202CB00003B/16

*9 780615 770123*